World Soccer Stars ⚽ Estrellas del fútbol mundial™

Gianluigi Buffon

Arturo Contró

English translation: Megan Benson

PowerKiDS press.™

Editorial Buenas Letras™
New York

Published in 2008 by The Rosen Publishing Group, Inc.
29 East 21st Street, New York, NY 10010

Copyright © 2008 by The Rosen Publishing Group, Inc.

First Edition
Book Design: Nelson Sa

Cataloging Data

Contró, Arturo, 1967-
   Gianluigi Buffon / Arturo Contró; English translation: Megan Benson — 1st ed.
     p.cm. – (World Soccer Stars / Estrellas del fútbol mundial).
   Includes Index.
   ISBN: 978-1-4042-7668-0
   1. Buffon, Gianluigi–Juvenile literature. 2. Soccer players–Biography–Juvenile
literature. 3. Spanish-language materials.

Manufactured in the United States of America

Photo Credits: Cover (left) © Franck Fife/Getty Images; cover (right) © Jacques Demarthon/Getty Images; p. 5 © Patrick Hertzog/Getty Images; pp. 7, 9 (top), 11 © Getty Images; p. 9 (bottom) © Patrik Stollarz/Getty Images; p. 13 © Ben Radford/Getty Images; p. 15 © Carlo Baroncini/Getty Images; p. 17 © AFP/Getty Images; p. 19 © Jochen Luebke/Getty Images; p. 21 © Grazia Neri/Getty Images.

Contents

Contenido

Gianluigi Buffon is a goalkeeper. On a soccer team, the goalkeeper's job is to keep the ball out of the **goal**.

Gianluigi Buffon juega como portero. En un equipo de fútbol, el portero se encarga de que el balón no entre en la **portería**.

Buffon has been named the best goalkeeper in the world for over 10 years. Buffon was born in Carrara, Italy, on January 28, 1978.

Durante más de diez años, Buffon ha sido llamado el mejor portero del mundo. Buffon nació en Carrara, Italia el 28 de enero de 1978.

Gianluigi Buffon, or "Gigi," as he is known, is 6 feet 3 inches (1.9 m) tall. His height helps him defend his team's goal.

Gianluigi Buffon, o "Gigi" como se le conoce, mide más de 6 pies, 3 pulgadas (1.9 m) de altura. Su altura le ayuda a defender la portería de su equipo.

6'6"
6'0"
5'6"
5'0"
4'6"
4'0"
3'6"
3'0"

RUI COSTA   SEBASTIÁN VERÓN   RAÚL   DAVID BECKHAM   RIVALDO   ROBERTO CARLOS   GIANLUIGI BUFFON

Buffon started playing soccer with the Italian team Parma AC in 1995.

Buffon empezó a jugar fútbol en el equipo Parma AC de Italia, en 1995.

In 2001, Buffon joined one of the best Italian teams, Juventus of Turin.
With this team, he became the most famous goalkeeper in the world.

En 2001, Buffon se unió a uno de los mejores equipos de Italia, el Juventus de Turín. En este equipo se convirtió en el portero más famoso del mundo.

Gigi is known for his great **reflexes**, which help him stop shots on goal. With Gigi as its goalkeeper, Juventus has been the Italian champion four times.

Gigi es conocido por sus **reflejos** para detener los tiros a gol. Con Gigi de portero, el Juventus ha sido 4 veces campeón de Italia.

Buffon has played in three **World Cups** with the Italian team. He played in France 1998, in Korea/Japan 2002, and in Germany 2006. Gigi won the World Cup Germany 2006 with the Italian team!

Buffon ha participado en tres **Copas del Mundo** con la selección de Italia. Gigi jugó en Francia 1998, en Corea-Japón 2002 y en Alemania 2006. ¡Gigi ganó la Copa del Mundo de Alemania 2006!

Gianluigi Buffon was named the best goalie of the World Cup in Germany 2006. Gigi allowed only two goals in seven games!

Gianluigi Buffon fue nombrado mejor portero de la Copa del Mundo en Alemania. ¡Gigi sólo recibió 2 goles en 7 partidos!

Soccer has given Gigi many special moments. Here he is meeting **Pope** John Paul II. The Pope gave Gigi a medal. Gigi gave the Pope his goalie gloves!

El fútbol le ha dado a Gigi muchos momentos especiales. Aquí, Gigi se encuentra con el **papa** Juan Pablo II. El papa le dió a Gigi una medalla. ¡Gigi le dió al papa sus guantes de portero!

21

Glossary / Glosario

goal (gohl) A frame with a net into which you aim a ball.

Pope (pohp) The person who leads the Roman Catholic Church.

reflexes (ree-fleksez**)** Fast movements. For a goalie, these movements help him stop the ball.

World Cup (wur-uld **kup)** A soccer tournament that takes place every four years with teams from around the world.

Copa del Mundo (la) Competencia de fútbol, cada 4 años, en la que juegan los mejores equipos del mundo.

papa (el) La persona que encabeza la Iglesia Católica.

portería (la) El lugar en un campo de fútbol formado por tres postes y una red en donde se anotan los goles.

reflejos (los) Un movimiento rápido. En el portero, este movimiento lo ayuda a detener el balón.

Resources / Recursos

Books in English/Libros en inglés

Otten, Jack. Soccer. New York: PowerKids
Press, 2002

Books in Spanish/Libros en español

Page, Jason. El fútbol. Minneapolis: Two-Can
Publishers, 2001

Web Sites

Due to the changing nature of Internet links, The
Rosen Publishing Group has developed an online
list of Web sites related to the subject of this book.
This site is updated regularly. Please use this link
to access the list:
www.buenasletraslinks.com/ss/buffon

Index

C
Carrara, Italy, 6

G
goal(s), 4, 8, 18
goalkeeper, 4, 6, 12,
    14

P
Parma, AC, 10
Pope John Paul II,
    20

J
Juventus of Turin, 12

W
World Cup(s), 16

Índice

C
Carrara, Italia, 6
Copas(s) del
    Mundo, 16

G
gol(es), 4, 8, 18

P
Parma, AC, 10
papa Juan Pablo II,
    20
portero, 4, 6, 12,
    14

J
Juventus de Turin,
    12